NIST Special Publication 800-147

BIOS Protection Guidelines

Recommendations of the National Institute of Standards and Technology

David Cooper
William Polk
Andrew Regenscheid
Murugiah Souppaya

C O M P U T E R   S E C U R I T Y

Computer Security Division
Information Technology Laboratory
National Institute of Standards and Technology
Gaithersburg, MD 20899-8930

April 2011

U.S. Department of Commerce

Gary Locke, Secretary

National Institute of Standards and Technology

Dr. Patrick D. Gallagher, Director

Reports on Computer Systems Technology

The Information Technology Laboratory (ITL) at the National Institute of Standards and Technology (NIST) promotes the U.S. economy and public welfare by providing technical leadership for the nation's measurement and standards infrastructure. ITL develops tests, test methods, reference data, proof of concept implementations, and technical analysis to advance the development and productive use of information technology. ITL's responsibilities include the development of technical, physical, administrative, and management standards and guidelines for the cost-effective security and privacy of sensitive unclassified information in Federal computer systems. This Special Publication 800-series reports on ITL's research, guidance, and outreach efforts in computer security and its collaborative activities with industry, government, and academic organizations.

National Institute of Standards and Technology Special Publication 800-147
Natl. Inst. Stand. Technol. Spec. Publ. 800-147, 27 pages (April 2011)

Acknowledgments

The authors, David Cooper, William Polk, Andrew Regenscheid, and Murugiah Souppaya of the National Institute of Standards and Technology (NIST) wish to thank their colleagues who reviewed drafts of this document and contributed to its technical content. The authors gratefully acknowledge and appreciate the contributions from individuals and organizations that submitted comments on the public draft of this publication. The comments and suggestions helped to improve the overall quality of the document.

In addition, the authors would also like to thank Gustavo Duarte, who created an earlier diagram of the boot-up process that was used as the basis for Figures 1 and 2 in this document.

Table of Contents

List of Appendices

Executive Summary

Modern computers rely on fundamental system firmware, commonly known as the system Basic Input/Output System (BIOS), to facilitate the hardware initialization process and transition control to the operating system. The BIOS is typically developed by both original equipment manufacturers (OEMs) and independent BIOS vendors, and is distributed to end-users by motherboard or computer manufacturers. Manufacturers frequently update system firmware to fix bugs, patch vulnerabilities, and support new hardware. This document provides security guidelines for preventing the unauthorized modification of BIOS firmware on PC client systems.

Unauthorized modification of BIOS firmware by malicious software constitutes a significant threat because of the BIOS's unique and privileged position within the PC architecture. A malicious BIOS modification could be part of a sophisticated, targeted attack on an organization—either a permanent denial of service (if the BIOS is corrupted) or a persistent malware presence (if the BIOS is implanted with malware). The move from conventional BIOS implementations to implementations based on the Unified Extensible Firmware Interface (UEFI) may make it easier for malware to target the BIOS in a widespread fashion, as these BIOS implementations are based on a common specification.

This document focuses on current and future x86 and x64 desktop and laptop systems, although the controls and procedures could potentially apply to any system design. Likewise, although the guide is oriented toward enterprise-class platforms, the necessary technologies are expected to migrate to consumer-grade systems over time. The security guidelines do not attempt to prevent installation of unauthentic BIOSs through the supply chain, by physical replacement of the BIOS chip, or through secure local update procedures.

Security guidelines are specified for four system BIOS features:
- The authenticated BIOS update mechanism, where digital signatures prevent the installation of BIOS update images that are not authentic.
- An optional secure local update mechanism, where physical presence authorizes installation of BIOS update images.
- Integrity protection features, to prevent unintended or malicious modification of the BIOS outside the authenticated BIOS update process.
- Non-bypassability features, to ensure that there are no mechanisms that allow the system processor or any other system component to bypass the authenticated update mechanism.

Additionally, management best practices which complement the security guidelines are presented. Five distinct phases are addressed:
- The Provisioning Phase, which establishes configuration baselines identifying the approved BIOS version and configuration settings.
- The Platform Deployment Phase, which establishes or verifies the configuration baseline using a secure local update mechanism.
- The Operations and Maintenance Phase, where systems are monitored for unexpected changes and planned BIOS updates are executed using the authenticated BIOS update mechanism.
- The Recovery Phase, which supports authorized rollback to an earlier BIOS version and recovery from a corrupted BIOS.
- The Disposition Phase, where the BIOS and configuration data are restored to their original settings to prevent against accidental information leakage.

Future revisions to this publication will also address the security of critical system firmware that interact with the BIOS.

1. Introduction

1.1 Authority

The National Institute of Standards and Technology (NIST) developed this document in furtherance of its statutory responsibilities under the Federal Information Security Management Act (FISMA) of 2002, Public Law 107-347.

NIST is responsible for developing standards and guidelines, including minimum requirements, for providing adequate information security for all agency operations and assets; but such standards and guidelines shall not apply to national security systems. This guideline is consistent with the requirements of the Office of Management and Budget (OMB) Circular A-130, Section 8b(3), "Securing Agency Information Systems," as analyzed in A-130, Appendix IV: Analysis of Key Sections. Supplemental information is provided in A-130, Appendix III.

This guideline has been prepared for use by Federal agencies. It may be used by nongovernmental organizations on a voluntary basis and is not subject to copyright, though attribution is desired.

Nothing in this document should be taken to contradict standards and guidelines made mandatory and binding on Federal agencies by the Secretary of Commerce under statutory authority, nor should these guidelines be interpreted as altering or superseding the existing authorities of the Secretary of Commerce, Director of the OMB, or any other Federal official.

1.2 Purpose and Scope

This document provides guidelines for preventing the unauthorized modification of *Basic Input/Output System (BIOS)* firmware on PC client systems. Unauthorized modification of BIOS firmware by malicious software constitutes a significant threat because of the BIOS's unique and privileged position within the PC architecture. A malicious BIOS modification could be part of a sophisticated, targeted attack on an organization —either a permanent denial of service (if the BIOS is corrupted) or a persistent malware presence (if the BIOS is implanted with malware).

As used in this publication, the term BIOS refers to conventional BIOS, *Extensible Firmware Interface (EFI)* BIOS, and *Unified Extensible Firmware Interface (UEFI)* BIOS. This document applies to system BIOS firmware (e.g., conventional BIOS or UEFI BIOS) stored in the system flash memory of computer systems, including portions that may be formatted as Option ROMs. However, it does not apply to Option ROMs, UEFI drivers, and firmware stored elsewhere in a computer system.

Section 3.1 of this guide provides platform vendors with recommendations and guidelines for a secure BIOS update process. Additionally, Section 3.2 provides recommendations for managing the BIOS in an operational environment. Future revisions to this publication will also address the security of critical system firmware that interact with the BIOS.

While this document focuses on current and future x86 and x64 client platforms, the controls and procedures are independent of any particular system design. Likewise, although the guide is oriented toward enterprise-class platforms, the necessary technologies are expected to migrate to consumer-grade systems over time. Future efforts may look at boot firmware security for enterprise server platforms.

1.3 Audience

The intended audience for this document includes BIOS and platform vendors, and information system security professionals who are responsible for managing the endpoint platforms' security, secure boot processes, and hardware security modules. The material may also be of use when developing enterprise-wide procurement strategies and deployment.

The material in this document is technically oriented, and it is assumed that readers have at least a basic understanding of system and network security. The document provides background information to help such readers understand the topics that are discussed. Readers are encouraged to take advantage of other resources (including those listed in this document) for more detailed information.

1.4 Document Structure

The remainder of this document is organized into the following major sections:

- Section 2 presents an overview of the BIOS and its role in the boot process, and identifies potential attacks against the BIOS in an operational environment.

- Section 3 examines how selected threats to the BIOS can be mitigated. Section 3.1 describes security controls for BIOS implementations that are required or recommended to mitigate these threats. Section 3.2 defines processes that leverage these controls to implement a secure BIOS update process within an enterprise as part of the platform management life cycle.

The document also contains appendices with supporting material:

- Appendix A contains a summary of the security guidelines for system BIOS implementations.

- Appendix B defines terms used in this document.

- Appendix C contains a list of acronyms and abbreviations used in this document.

- Appendix D contains a list of references used in the development of this document.

2. Background

Modern computers such as desktop and laptop computers contain program code that facilitates the hardware initialization process. The code is stored in non-volatile memory and is commonly referred to as boot firmware. The primary firmware used to initialize the system is called the *Basic Input/Output System (BIOS)* or the *system BIOS*. This section provides background information on the system BIOS and its role in the boot process using the conventional BIOS and Unified Extensible Firmware Interface (UEFI) BIOS as examples. It identifies the primary methods used for updating the system BIOS, and security issues and threats to the system BIOS.

2.1 System BIOS

The system BIOS is the first piece of software executed on the main central processing unit (CPU) when a computer is powered on. While the system BIOS was originally responsible for providing operating systems access to hardware, its primary role on modern machines is to initialize and test hardware components and load the operating system. In addition, the BIOS loads and initializes important system management functions, such as power and thermal management. The system BIOS may also load CPU microcode patches during the boot process.

There are several different types of BIOS firmware. Some computers use a 16-bit conventional BIOS, while many newer systems use boot firmware based on the UEFI specifications [UEFI]. In this document we refer to all types of boot firmware as BIOS firmware, the system BIOS, or simply BIOS. When necessary, we differentiate conventional BIOS firmware from UEFI firmware by calling them the conventional BIOS and UEFI BIOS, respectively.

System BIOS is typically developed by both original equipment manufacturers (OEMs) and independent BIOS vendors, and is distributed to end users with computer hardware. Manufacturers frequently update system firmware to fix bugs, patch vulnerabilities, and support new hardware. The system BIOS is typically stored on electrically erasable programmable read-only memory (EEPROM) or other forms of flash memory, and is modifiable by end users. Typically, system BIOS firmware is updated using a utility or tool that has special knowledge of the non-volatile storage components in which the BIOS is stored.

A given computer system can have BIOS in several different locations. In addition to the motherboard, BIOS can be found on hard drive controllers, video cards, network cards and other add-in cards. This additional firmware generally takes the form of *Option ROMs* (containing conventional BIOS and/or UEFI drivers). These are loaded and executed by the system firmware during the boot process. Other system devices, such as hard drives and optical drives, may have their own microcontrollers and other types of firmware.

As noted in Section 1.2, the guidelines in this document apply BIOS firmware stored in the system flash. This includes Option ROMs and UEFI drivers that are stored with the system BIOS firmware and are updated by the same mechanism. It does not apply to Option ROMs, UEFI drivers, and firmware stored elsewhere in a computer system.

2.2 Role of System BIOS in the Boot Process

The primary function of the system BIOS is to initialize important hardware components and to load the operating system. This process is known as *booting*. The boot process of the system BIOS typically executes in the following stages:

1. **Execute Core Root of Trust:** The system BIOS may include a small core block of firmware that executes first and is capable of verifying the integrity of other firmware components. This has traditionally been called the *BIOS Boot Block*. For trusted computing applications, it may also contain the Core Root of Trust for Measurement (CRTM).
2. **Initialize and Test Low-Level Hardware:** Very early in the boot process the system BIOS initializes and tests key pieces of hardware on the computer system, including the motherboard, chipset, memory and CPU.
3. **Load and Execute Additional Firmware Modules:** The system BIOS executes additional pieces of firmware that either extend the capabilities of the system BIOS or initialize other hardware components necessary for booting the system. These additional modules may be stored within the same flash memory as the system BIOS or they may be stored in the hardware devices they initialize (e.g., video card, local area network card).
4. **Select Boot Device:** After system hardware has been configured, the system BIOS searches for a boot device (e.g., hard drive, optical drive, USB drive) and executes the boot loader stored on that device.
5. **Load Operating System**: While the system BIOS is still in control of the computer, the boot loader begins to load and initialize the operating system kernel. Once the kernel is functional, primary control of the computer system transfers from the system BIOS to the operating system.

In addition, the system BIOS loads system management interrupt (SMI) handlers (also known as System Management Mode (SMM) code) and initializes Advanced Configuration and Power Interface (ACPI) tables and code. These provide important system management functions for the running computer system, such as power and thermal management.

This section describes the boot process in conventional BIOS-based systems and the boot process in UEFI-based systems. While conventional BIOS is used in many desktop and laptop computers deployed today, the industry has begun transitioning to UEFI BIOS.

2.2.1 Conventional BIOS Boot Process

Figure 1 shows a typical boot process for x86-compatible systems running a conventional BIOS. The conventional BIOS often executes in 16-bit real mode, although some more recent implementations execute in protected mode. Some conventional BIOS-based firmware has a small block of BIOS firmware— known as the BIOS boot block— that is logically separate from the rest of the BIOS. On these computer systems, the boot block is the first firmware executed during the boot process. The boot block is responsible for checking the integrity of the remaining BIOS code, and may provide mechanisms for recovery if the main system BIOS firmware is corrupted. On most trusted computing architectures, the BIOS boot block serves as the computer system's CRTM because this firmware is implicitly trusted to bootstrap the process of building a measurement chain for subsequent attestation of other firmware and software that is executed on the machine [TCG05].

The boot block executes the part of the conventional BIOS that initializes most hardware components— the *Power-on-Self-Test* (POST) code. During POST, key low-level hardware on the computer system is initialized, including the chipset, CPU, and memory. The system BIOS initializes the video card, which may load and execute its own BIOS to initialize graphics processors and memory.

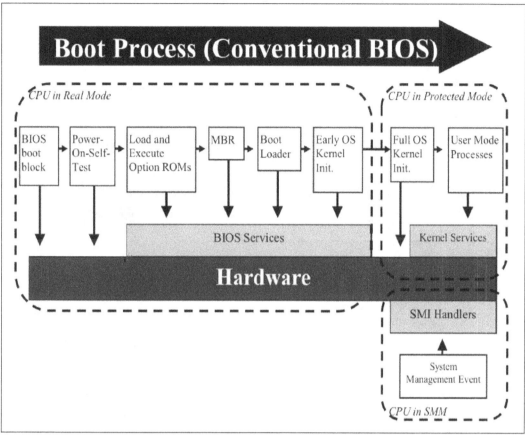

Figure 1: Conventional BIOS Boot Process[1]

Next, the system BIOS searches for other peripherals and microcontrollers, and executes any Option ROMs on these components necessary to initialize them. Option ROMs execute very early in the boot process and can add a variety of features to the boot process. For example, the Option ROM on a network adapter could load the Preboot Execution Environment (PXE), which allows a computer to boot over the network.

Next, the system BIOS scans the computer system for storage devices that have been identified as boot devices. In a typical case, the BIOS attempts to boot from the first boot device it finds that has a valid master boot record (MBR). The MBR points to a boot loader stored on the hard drive, which in turn starts the process of loading the operating system.

During the boot process the system BIOS loads SMI handlers and initializes ACPI tables and code. SMI handlers run in a special high-privilege mode on the CPU known as System Management Mode, a 32-bit mode that is capable of bypassing many of the hardware security mechanisms of protected mode, such as memory segmentation and page protections.

---

[1] This figure is based on information and a diagram found at [Duarte08].

2.2.2   UEFI Boot Process

At a high level, the UEFI boot process, shown in Figure 2, follows a similar flow to the conventional BIOS boot process. One difference is that UEFI code runs in 32- or 64-bit protected mode on the CPU, not in 16-bit real mode as is often the case with conventional BIOS. Most UEFI-based platforms start with a small core block of code that has the primary responsibility of authenticating subsequent code executed on the computer system. This is very similar to the role of the boot block in conventional BIOS. This part of the boot process is known as the Security (SEC) phase, and it serves as the core root of trust in the computer system.

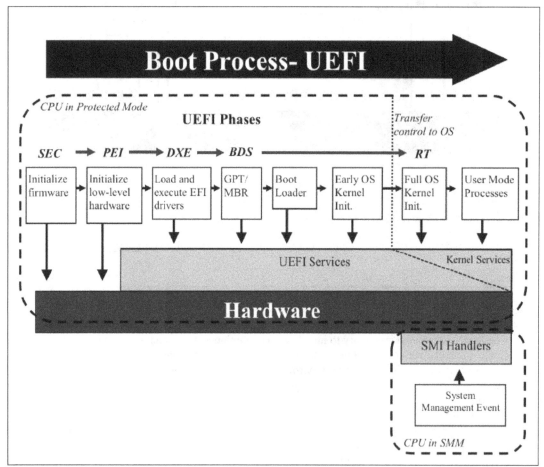

Figure 2: UEFI BIOS Boot Process

The next phase of the UEFI boot process is the Pre-EFI Initialization (PEI) Phase. The PEI phase is intended to initialize key system components, such as the processor, chipset and motherboard. In some cases, the code in the Security Phase and the PEI Phase comprise the core root of trust in a UEFI system.

The purpose of the PEI Phase is to prepare the system for the Driver Execution Environment (DXE) phase. The DXE phase is where most system initialization is performed. The firmware executed in this phase is responsible for searching for and executing drivers that provide device support during the boot process, or provide additional features. During this phase the UEFI BIOS may execute conventional option ROMs, which have a similar purpose.

The PEI and DXE phases of the UEFI boot process lay the foundation to load an operating system. The final tasks necessary to load an operating system are performed in the Boot Device Selection (BDS) phase. This phase initializes console devices for simple input/output operations on the system. These console devices include local text or graphical interfaces, as well as remote interfaces, such as Telnet or remote displays over HTTP. The BDS phase also loads any additional drivers necessary to manage console or boot devices. Finally, the firmware loads the boot loader from the first MBR or GUID Partition Table (GPT) formatted boot device, and loads the operating system.

During the boot process the UEFI BIOS loads SMI handlers and initializes ACPI tables and code.

The Run Time phase of the UEFI boot process begins when the operating system is ready to take control from the UEFI BIOS. UEFI runtime services are available to the operating system during this phase.

2.3   Updating the System BIOS

A system and its supporting management software and firmware may provide several authorized mechanisms for legitimately updating the system BIOS. These include:

1. **User-Initiated Updates:** System and motherboard manufacturers typically supply end users with utilities capable of updating the system BIOS. Historically, end users booted from external media to perform these updates, but today most manufacturers provide utilities that can update the system BIOS from the user's normal operating system. Depending on the security mechanisms implemented on the system, these utilities might directly update the system BIOS or they may schedule an update for the next system reboot.
2. **Managed Updates:** A given computer system may have hardware and software-based agents that allow a system administrator to remotely update the system BIOS without direct involvement from the user.
3. **Rollback:** System BIOS implementations that authenticate updates before applying them may also check version numbers during the update process. In these cases, the system BIOS may have a special update process for rolling back the installed firmware to an earlier version. For instance, the rollback process might require the physical presence of the user. This mechanism guards against attackers flashing old firmware with known vulnerabilities.
4. **Manual Recovery:** To recover from a corrupt or malfunctioning system BIOS, many computer systems provide mechanisms to allow a user with physical presence during the boot process to replace the current system BIOS with a known good version and configuration.
5. **Automatic Recovery:** Some computer systems are able to detect when the system BIOS has been corrupted and recover from a backup firmware image stored in a separate storage location from the primary system BIOS (e.g., a second flash memory chip, a hidden partition on a hard drive).

2.4   Importance of BIOS Integrity

As the first code that is executed by the main CPU, the system BIOS is a critical security component of a computer system. While the system BIOS, possibly with the use of a Trusted Platform Module (TPM), can verify the integrity of firmware and software executed later in the boot process, typically all or part of the system BIOS is implicitly trusted.

The system BIOS is a potentially attractive target for attack. Malicious code running at the BIOS level could have a great deal of control over a computer system. It could be used to compromise any components that are loaded later in the boot process, including the SMM code, boot loader, hypervisor, and operating system. The BIOS is stored on non-volatile memory that persists between power cycles. Malware written into a BIOS could be used to re-infect machines even after new operating systems have been installed or hard drives replaced. Because the system BIOS runs early in the boot process with very high privileges on the machine, malware running at the BIOS level may be very difficult to detect. Because the BIOS loads first, there is no opportunity for anti-malware products to authoritatively scan the BIOS.

BIOS exploits would likely be highly system-specific—directed at a specific version of a system BIOS or certain hardware components (e.g., a particular motherboard chipset). In contrast, most malware targets software executing at or above the operating system kernel, where it is easier to develop and can attack larger classes of machines. BIOS-level malware may be more likely employed in targeted attacks on high-value computer systems. The move to UEFI-based BIOS may make it easier for malware to target the BIOS in a widespread fashion, as these BIOS implementations are based on a common specification.

For the reasons outlined above, there are few known instances of BIOS-level malware. At this time, the only publicly known malware targeting the system BIOS that has infected a significant number of computers is the CIH virus, also known as the Chernobyl virus [Sym02], first discovered in 1998. One element of the payload of this virus attempted to overwrite the BIOS on systems using a specific chipset that was widely deployed at the time. This malware relied on several vulnerabilities that are not present in modern machines.

Security researchers have demonstrated other potential attacks on conventional BIOS and EFI/UEFI firmware. Proof-of-concept attacks have been demonstrated that allow for the insertion of malicious code into conventional BIOS implementations that permit unsigned updates [SaOr09]. Other researchers have discovered a buffer-overflow vulnerability in the EFI BIOS on a modern platform. Although this EFI BIOS write-protects firmware early in the boot process and only flashes signed updates to firmware, the buffer overflow allowed the researchers to bypass the secure update process by executing an unsigned portion of the firmware update package before write protections were applied [WoTe09].

Vulnerabilities such as these could allow attackers to create stealthy malware that operate with very high privileges on a system. The system BIOS loads SMI handlers before passing control of the computer to the operating system. Malicious code written into a BIOS could modify the SMI handlers to create malware that would run in SMM [EmSp08]. This would give the malware unrestricted access to physical memory and peripherals connected to the host machine, and it would be very difficult for software running on the operating system to detect.

2.5   Threats to the System BIOS

The preceding section established the importance of maintaining the integrity of the system BIOS. This section describes some of the various ways that the integrity of the system BIOS can be attacked, and identifies the attacks considered within scope for the security controls and processes specified in Section 3.

The first threat to the integrity of the system BIOS comes while the system moves through the supply chain. Supply chain security techniques are out of scope for the security controls specified in this document. Some of the procedures specified in Section 3.2 can, however, be used to identify and remedy systems that have an unapproved system BIOS.

Assuming that the system arrives with the manufacturer's intended system BIOS installed, there are a number of threats to the integrity of the system BIOS during the system's lifetime:

- One of the most difficult threats to prevent is a user-initiated installation of a malicious system BIOS. User-initiated BIOS update utilities are often the primary method for updating the system BIOS. The guidelines included in this document will not prevent users from installing unapproved BIOS images if they have physical access to the computer system. As with supply chain threats, security processes may be able to detect and remediate the unapproved system BIOS, such as initiating a recovery process to restore to an approved BIOS.

- Malware could leverage weak BIOS security controls or exploit vulnerabilities in the system BIOS itself to reflash or modify the system BIOS. General-purpose malicious software is unlikely to include this functionality, but a targeted attack on an organization could be directed towards an organization's standard system BIOS. The malicious BIOS can be delivered to the system either over a network, or using media. The guidelines presented in this document are designed to prevent these kinds of attack.

- Network-based system management tools could also be used to launch an organization-wide attack on system BIOSs. For example, consider an organization-maintained update server for the organization's deployed system BIOS; a compromised server could push a malicious system BIOS to computer systems across the organization. This is a high-impact attack, but requires either an insider or compromise of an organization's update process. The guidelines presented in this document are designed to prevent this kind of attack.

- Any of the preceding mechanisms could be used to rollback to an authentic but vulnerable system BIOS. This is a particularly insidious attack, since the "bad" BIOS is authentic (i.e., shipped by the manufacturer). The security controls specified in the following section are primarily focused on verifying the source and integrity of the system BIOS. This document includes recommended controls for rollback protection.

The controls described in the following section are primarily focused on preventing unauthorized modification of the system BIOS by potentially malicious software running on computer systems. Installation of an unapproved system BIOS in the supply chain, by individuals with physical access, or through rollback to an authenticated but vulnerable system BIOS, are not addressed by the controls in Section 3.1, but can be addressed using processes specified in Section 3.2.

3. Threat Mitigation

BIOS is a critical component of a secure system. As the first code executed during the boot process, the system BIOS is implicitly trusted by hardware and software components in a system. The previous section described the system BIOS's role in the boot process, the system BIOS's appeal to attackers, and the potential threats resulting in the unauthorized modification of the BIOS. This section presents security guidelines for BIOS implementations and recommended practices for managing BIOSs in an enterprise environment. Section 3.1 provides guidelines for a secure BIOS update process. It is intended for platform vendors designing, implementing, or selecting a system BIOS implementation. While products may not be immediately available, organizations can use these guidelines at input to their procurement processes and begin developing plans to make use of these security features when they are available. Organizations can use the recommended BIOS management practices in Section 3.2 when developing these plans. The recommendations are intended to prevent unauthorized modification of the BIOS.

3.1 Security Guidelines for System BIOS Implementations

This subsection provides guidelines intended to maintain the integrity of the BIOS after it has been provisioned by securing the mechanisms used for updating the BIOS. In particular, this subsection defines guidelines for system BIOS implementations for a secure BIOS update mechanism. A secure BIOS update mechanism includes:

1. a process for verifying the authenticity and integrity of BIOS updates; and
2. a mechanism for ensuring that the BIOS is protected from modification outside of the secure update process.

Authentication verifies that a BIOS update image was generated by an authentic source and is unaltered. All updates to the system BIOS shall either go through an authenticated BIOS update mechanism as described in Section 3.1.1 or use an optional secure local update mechanism compliant with the guidelines in Section 3.1.2.

These guidelines for a secure BIOS update mechanism do not mitigate all risks associated with the system BIOS. Some threats to unauthorized modification of the system BIOS remain. For example, these guidelines do not prevent individuals with physical access to systems from modifying the system BIOS. Nor do they guarantee the absence of vulnerabilities in the system BIOS implementations. The guidelines on the system BIOS should be used in conjunction with organizations' existing security policies and procedures.

3.1.1 BIOS Update Authentication

The authenticated BIOS update mechanism employs digital signatures to ensure the authenticity of the BIOS update image. To update the BIOS using the authenticated BIOS update mechanism, there shall be a Root of Trust for Update (RTU) that contains a signature verification algorithm and a key store that includes the public key needed to verify the signature on the BIOS update image. The key store and the signature verification algorithm shall be stored in a protected fashion on the computer system and shall be modifiable only using an authenticated update mechanism or a secure local update mechanism as outlined in Section 3.1.2.

The key store in the RTU shall include a public key used to verify the signature on a BIOS update image or include a hash [FIPS 180-3] of the public key if a copy of the public key is provided with the BIOS update image. In the latter case, the update mechanism shall hash the public key provided with the BIOS update image and ensure that it matches a hash which appears in the key store before using the provided public key to verify the signature on the BIOS update image.

BIOS images shall be signed in conformance with NIST SP 800-89, *Recommendation for Obtaining Assurances for Digital Signature Applications* [SP800-89], using an approved digital signature algorithm as specified in NIST FIPS 186-3, *Digital Signature Standard* [FIPS186-3], that provides at least 112 bits of security strength, in accordance with NIST SP 800-131A, *Transitions: Recommendation for Transitioning the Use of Cryptographic Algorithms and Key Lengths* [SP800-131A].

The update mechanism shall ensure that the BIOS update image has been digitally signed and that the digital signature can be verified using a key in the RTU before updating the BIOS. Recovery mechanisms shall also use the authenticated update mechanism unless the recovery process meets the guidelines for a secure local update. The authenticated update mechanism should prevent the unauthorized rollback of the BIOS to an earlier authentic version that has a known security weakness. This limitation of the rollback mechanism may be accomplished, for example, by verifying that the version number of the BIOS image is larger than the currently installed BIOS image's version number.

Some organizations may wish to assert greater control over BIOS updates in high-security environments. The authenticated update mechanism may be designed to permit organizational control over the update process, where updates to the BIOS or rollbacks of the BIOS to an earlier version are permitted only if the update or rollback has been authorized by the organization. For example, specific BIOS images could be authorized by an organization by countersigning them with an organization-controlled key, which would be verified during the update process.

3.1.2   Secure Local Update

BIOS implementations may optionally include a secure local update mechanism that updates the system BIOS without using the authenticated update mechanism. The secure local update mechanism, if it is implemented, should be used only to load the first BIOS image or to recover from a corruption of a system BIOS that cannot be fixed using the authenticated update mechanism described in Section 3.1.1. A secure local update mechanism shall ensure the authenticity and integrity of the BIOS update image by requiring physical presence. Further protections may be implemented in the secure local update mechanism by requiring the entry of an administrator password or the unlocking of a physical lock (e.g., a motherboard jumper) before permitting the system BIOS to be updated.

3.1.3   Integrity Protection

To prevent unintended or malicious modification of the system BIOS outside the authenticated BIOS update process, the RTU and the system BIOS (excluding configuration data used by the system BIOS that is stored in non-volatile memory) shall be protected from unintended or malicious modification with a mechanism that cannot be overridden outside of an authenticated BIOS update. The protection mechanism shall itself be protected from unauthorized modification.

The authenticated BIOS update mechanism shall be protected from unintended or malicious modification by a mechanism that is at least as strong as that protecting the RTU and the system BIOS.

The protection mechanism shall protect relevant regions of the system flash memory containing the system BIOS prior to executing firmware or software that can be modified without using an authenticated update mechanism or a secure local update mechanism. Protections should be enforced by hardware mechanisms that are not alterable except by an authorized mechanism.

3.1.4 Non-Bypassability

The authenticated BIOS update mechanism shall be the exclusive mechanism for modifying the system BIOS absent physical intervention through the secure local update mechanism. The design of the system and accompanying system components and firmware shall ensure that there are no mechanisms that allow the system processor or any other system component to bypass the authenticated update mechanism, except for the secure local update mechanism. Any such mechanisms capable of bypassing the authenticated update mechanism could create a vulnerability allowing malicious software to modify the system BIOS or overwrite the system flash with a BIOS image from an illegitimate source.

A modern platform includes design features that give system components direct access to the system BIOS for performance improvements, such as shadowing the BIOS in RAM or for system management mode operations. System components may have read access to BIOS flash memory, but they shall not be able to directly modify the system BIOS except through the authenticated update mechanism or by an authorized mechanism requiring physical intervention. For example, bus mastering that bypasses the main processor (e.g., Direct Memory Access to the system flash) shall not be capable of directly modifying the firmware. Also, microcontrollers on the system shall not be capable of directly modifying the firmware, unless the hardware and firmware components of the microcontroller are protected with equivalent mechanisms at the RTU. These non-bypassability guidelines do not apply to configuration data used by the system BIOS that is stored in non-volatile memory.

3.2 Recommended Practices for BIOS Management

This section introduces considerations for managing system BIOS in an enterprise operational environment leveraging the existing policy, process, and operations practices. It focuses on key activities revolving around provisioning, deploying, managing, and decommissioning the system BIOS as part of its overall platform life cycle. Activities performed in a recovery phase are also specified to handle exceptional conditions.

Provisioning Phase: It is crucial that the organization institute a mechanism for identifying, inventorying, and tracking the different computer systems across the enterprise throughout their life cycle. Identifying and monitoring the BIOS image characteristics such as manufacturer name, version, or time stamp allows the organization to perform update, rollback, and recovery. The organization should maintain a "golden master image" for each approved system BIOS, including superseded versions, in secure offline storage.

If the platform has a configurable Root of Trust for Update (RTU), the organization needs to maintain a copy of the key store and signature verification algorithm. If the RTU is integrated into the system BIOS then this guideline is satisfied by maintaining the golden BIOS image. If the RTU is not integrated into the system BIOS, the security afforded the RTU should be at least as strong as that for the golden BIOS image.

Most organizations will rely upon the manufacturer as the source for the authenticated BIOS. In this case, the organization does not maintain any private keys, and the RTU contains only public keys provided by the manufacturer. Where the organization prefers to participate actively in the BIOS authentication process by countersigning some or all approved system BIOS updates, the RTU may contain one or more public keys associated with the organization. In this case, the organization must securely maintain the corresponding private key so that the next BIOS update can be signed. Private keys should be maintained under multi-party control to protect against insider attacks. For organizational keys, the corresponding public keys must also be maintained securely (to ensure authentication of origin).

In addition, a common configuration baseline for each platform must be created to conform to the organization's policy. The baseline should ensure that the integrity protection and non-bypassability features are enabled (if they are configurable), and organization policies for password policy and device boot order are enforced. Finally, the BIOS image information and associated baseline of settings for each platform should be documented in the configuration management plan.[2]

Platform Deployment Phase: The secure local update process should be used to provision the approved BIOS for that platform from the golden master image, the corresponding RTU should be installed, and BIOS-related configuration parameters established before computer systems are deployed. This will help the organization maintain a consistent, known starting posture. The organization should periodically perform assessments to confirm that the organization's BIOS policies, processes, and procedures are being followed properly.

Specifically, the procedures must ensure that the appropriate system BIOS is installed, the RTU contains all required keys and no unauthorized keys, and the integrity protection and non-bypassability features are enabled if they are configurable.

Operation and Maintenance Phase: This phase includes the operations and maintenance activities that are important for maintaining BIOS security and reliability in the operational environment. System BIOS updates should be performed using a change management process and the new approved version should be documented in the configuration plan, noting the previous BIOS image has been superseded.

The BIOS image and configuration baseline should be continuously monitored. If an unapproved deviation from this baseline is detected, the event should be investigated, documented, and remediated as part of incident response activities. The incident response plan should document the process and set of authorized tools that can be used to capture the evidence to help determine the root cause.[3] The secure local update mechanism should be used to recover from a BIOS image compromise.

When a new BIOS image is required to extend system capabilities, improve system reliability, or remediate software vulnerabilities, BIOS updates should be performed using the authenticated update process. Where the organization participates actively in the update process, the multi-party control process must be executed to retrieve the private key from secure storage and generate the digital signature. The BIOS installation package should also be signed, and the digital signature should be verified before execution. Once the update has executed successfully, the configuration baseline should be validated to confirm that the computer system is still in compliance with the organization's defined policy.

Recovery Phase: In some circumstances, a BIOS update will be required that cannot be accomplished using the authenticated update process. For example, a corrupted system BIOS or RTU may be unable to execute or invoke the authentication procedures. In this case, the appropriate system BIOS and/or RTU may be able to be installed using the secure local update process. In other cases, a BIOS update may have unintended consequences, forcing the organization to roll back to an earlier version. Extra steps may be required for an authenticated update to authorize rollback (if versioning or timestamps are compared during the standard authentication process), or the secure local update process may be required to reestablish a secure baseline. As with the Operations and Maintenance phase, it is essential to validate

---

[2] See Draft NIST SP 800-128, *Guide for Security Configuration Management of Information Systems* [SP800-128] for guidelines on developing a configuration management plan.
[3] For additional information on establishing incident response capabilities and handling incidents efficiently and effectively, see NIST SP 800-61rev1 *Computer Security Incident Handling Guide* [SP800-61].

the configuration of the BIOS against the organization's defined policy after BIOS rollback or reinstallation.

Disposition Phase: Before the computer system is disposed and leaves the organization, the organization should remove or destroy any sensitive data from the system BIOS. The configuration baseline should be reset to the manufacturer's default profile; in particular, sensitive settings such as passwords should be deleted from the system and keys should also be removed from the key store. If the system BIOS includes any organization-specific customizations then a vendor-provided BIOS image should be installed. This phase of the platform life cycle reduces chances for accidental data leakage.

Appendix A   Summary of Guidelines for System BIOS Implementations

This appendix contains a summary of the secure BIOS update guidelines for system BIOS implementations found in Section 3.1. These guidelines are intended for platform vendors designing, implementing, or selecting a system BIOS implementation. Readers should consult the relevant sections in the main body of this document for additional informative text that further describes the intent and context of the guidelines.

1. Approved BIOS Update Mechanisms

1-A   All updates to the system BIOS shall use either an authenticated BIOS update mechanism as described in Section 3.1.1 or an optional secure local update mechanism compliant with the guidelines in Section 3.1.2.

2. BIOS Update Authentication

2-A   There shall be a Root of Trust for Update (RTU) that contains a signature verification algorithm and a key store that includes the public key needed to verify the signature on the BIOS update image.

2-B   The key store and the signature verification algorithm shall be stored in a protected fashion on the computer system and shall be modifiable only using an authenticated update mechanism or a secure local update mechanism as outlined in Section 3.1.2.

2-C   The key store in the RTU shall include the public key for verifying the signature on a BIOS update image or include the hash [FIPS 180-3] of the public key for verifying the signature on a BIOS update image that includes the public key. In the latter case, the update mechanism shall ensure that the hash of the public key provided with the BIOS update image appears in the key store before using the provided public key to verify the signature on the BIOS update image.

2-D   BIOS images shall be signed in conformance with NIST SP 800-89, *Recommendation for Obtaining Assurances for Digital Signature Applications* [SP800-89], using an approved digital signature algorithm as specified in NIST FIPS 186-3, *Digital Signature Standard* [FIPS186-3], that provides at least 112 bits of security strength, in accordance with NIST SP 800-131A, *Transitions: Recommendation for Transitioning the Use of Cryptographic Algorithms and Key Lengths* [SP800-131A].

2-E   The authenticated update mechanism shall ensure that the BIOS update image has been digitally signed and that the digital signature can be verified using one of the keys in the key store in the RTU before updating the BIOS.

3. Secure Local Update (Optional)

BIOS implementations may optionally include a secure local update mechanism, where physical presence authorizes installation of BIOS update images without necessarily using the authenticate update mechanism.

3-A   A secure local update mechanism shall ensure the authenticity and integrity of the BIOS update image by requiring physical presence.

4. Integrity Protection

4-A The RTU and the BIOS (excluding configuration data used by the BIOS that is stored in non-volatile memory) shall be protected from unintended or malicious modification using a mechanism that cannot be overridden outside of an authenticated BIOS update.

4-B The protection mechanism shall be protected from unauthorized modification.

4-C The authenticated BIOS update mechanism shall be protected from unintended or malicious modification by a mechanism that is at least as strong as that protecting the RTU and the system BIOS.

4-D The protection mechanism shall protect relevant regions of the system flash memory containing the system BIOS prior to executing firmware or software that can be modified without using an authenticated update mechanism or a secure local update mechanism.

4-E Protections should be enforced by hardware mechanisms that are not alterable except by an authorized mechanism.

5. Non-Bypassability

These non-bypassability guidelines do not apply to configuration data used by the system BIOS that is stored in non-volatile memory.

5-A The authenticated BIOS update mechanism shall be the exclusive mechanism for modifying the system BIOS absent physical intervention through the secure local update mechanism.

5-B The design of the system and accompanying system components and firmware shall ensure that there are no mechanisms that allow the system processor or any other system component to bypass the authenticated update mechanism, except for the secure local update mechanism.

5-C While system components may have read access to BIOS flash memory, they shall not be able to directly modify the system BIOS except through the authenticated update mechanism or by an authorized mechanism requiring physical intervention.

5-C.i Bus mastering that bypasses the main processor (e.g., Direct Memory Access to the system flash) shall not be capable of directly modifying the firmware.

Microcontrollers on the system shall not be capable of directly modifying the firmware, unless the hardware and firmware components of the microcontroller are protected with equivalent mechanisms at the RTU.

Appendix B   Glossary

Selected terms used in the publication are defined below.

Basic Input/Output System (BIOS): In this publication, refers collectively to boot firmware based on the conventional BIOS, Extensible Firmware Interface (EFI), and the Unified Extensible Firmware Interface (UEFI).

Conventional BIOS: Legacy boot firmware used in many x86-compatible computer systems. Also known as the legacy BIOS.

Core Root of Trust for Measurement (CRTM): The first piece of BIOS code that executes on the main processor during the boot process. On a system with a Trusted Platform Module the CRTM is implicitly trusted to bootstrap the process of building a measurement chain for subsequent attestation of other firmware and software that is executed on the computer system.

Extensible Firmware Interface (EFI): A specification for the interface between the operating system and the platform firmware. Version 1.10 of the EFI specifications was the final version of the EFI specifications, and subsequent revisions made by the Unified EFI Forum are part of the UEFI specifications.

Firmware: Software that is included in read-only memory (ROM).

Option ROM: Firmware that is called by the system BIOS. Option ROMs include BIOS firmware on add-on cards (e.g., video card, hard drive controller, network card) as well as modules which extend the capabilities of the system BIOS.

Protected Mode: An operational mode found in x86-compatible processors with hardware support for memory protection, virtual memory, and multitasking.

Real Mode: A legacy high-privilege operating mode in x86-compatible processors.

System Management Mode (SMM): A high-privilege operating mode found in x86-compatible processors used for low-level system management functions. System Management Mode is only entered after the system generates a System Management Interrupt and only executes code from a segregated block of memory.

System Flash Memory: The non-volatile storage location of system BIOS, typically in electronically erasable programmable read-only memory (EEPROM) flash memory on the motherboard. While system flash memory is a technology-specific term, guidelines in this document referring to the system flash memory are intended to apply to any non-volatile storage medium containing the system BIOS.

Trusted Platform Module (TPM): A tamper-resistant integrated circuit built into some computer motherboards that can perform cryptographic operations (including key generation) and protect small amounts of sensitive information, such as passwords and cryptographic keys.

Unified Extensible Firmware Interface (UEFI): A possible replacement for the conventional BIOS that is becoming widely deployed in new x86-based computer systems. The UEFI specifications were preceded by the EFI specifications.

Appendix C Acronyms and Abbreviations

This appendix contains a list of selected acronyms and abbreviations used in the guide.

ACPI	Advanced Configuration and Power Interface
BDS	Boot Device Selection
BIOS	Basic Input/Output System
CPU	Central Processing Unit
CRTM	Core Root of Trust for Measurement
DXE	Driver Execution Environment
EEPROM	Electrically Erasable Programmable Read-Only Memory
EFI	Extensible Firmware Interface
FIPS	Federal Information Processing Standard
FISMA	Federal Information Security Management Act
GPT	GUID Partition Table
GUID	Globally Unique Identifier
HTTP	Hypertext Transfer Protocol
IT	Information Technology
ITL	Information Technology Laboratory
MBR	Master Boot Record
NIST	National Institute of Standards and Technology
OEM	Original Equipment Manufacturer
OMB	Office of Management and Budget
OS	Operating System
PEI	Pre-EFI Initialization
POST	Power-on self-test
PXE	Preboot Execution Environment
ROM	Read-only Memory
RT	Runtime
RTU	Root of Trust for Update
SMI	System Management Interrupt
SMM	System Management Mode
SP	Special Publication
TPM	Trusted Platform Module
UEFI	Unified Extensible Firmware Interface

Appendix D References

The list below provides references for this publication.

[Duarte08]   G. Duarte. "How Computers Boot Up." 5 June 2008.
              http://www.duartes.org/gustavo/blog/post/how-computers-boot-up

[EFI]   *EFI 1.10 Specification*. Intel. 1 November 2003. http://www.intel.com/technology/efi/

[EmSp08]   Shawn Embleton, Sherri Sparks, and Cliff C. Zou. "SMM Rootkits: A New Breed of OS
              Independent Malware," *Proceedings of 4th International Conference on Security and
              Privacy in Communication Networks (SecureComm)*, Istanbul, Turkey, September 22-25,
              2008.

[FIPS180-3]   FIPS 180-3, *Secure Hash Standard*. October 2008.

[FIPS186-3]   FIPS 186-3, *Digital Signature Standard*. June 2009.

[DuGr09]   Loïc Duflot, Olivier Grumelard, Olivier Levillain and Benjamin Morin. "ACPI and SMI
              handlers: some limits to trusted computing." *Journal in Computer Virology*. Volume 6,
              Number 4, 353-374.

[Graw09]   D. Grawrock. *Dynamics of a Trusted Platform: A Building Block Approach*. Hillsboro,
              OR: Intel Press, 2009.

[Heas07a]   J. Heasman. "Firmware Rootkits: A Threat to the Enterprise." Black Hat DC.
              Washington, DC. 28 February 2007.
              http://www.nccgroup.com/Libraries/Document_Downloads/02_07_Firmware_Rootkits
              _The_Threat_to_the_Enterprise_Black_Hat_Washington_2007_sflb.sflb.ashx

[Heas07b]   J. Heasman. "Hacking the Extensible Firmware Interface." *Black Hat USA*. Las Vegas,
              NV. 2 August 2007. https://www.blackhat.com/presentations/bh-usa-
              07/Heasman/Presentation/bh-usa-07-heasman.pdf

[Intel03]   *Intel Platform Innovation Framework for EFI- Architecture Specification v0.9*. Intel.
              September 2003. http://www.intel.com/technology/framework/

[KGH09]   A. Kumar, G. Purushottam, and Y. Saint-Hilaire. *Active Platform Management
              Demystified*. Hillsboro, OR: Intel Press, 2009.

[Sal07]   Salihun, Darmawan. *BIOS Disassembly Ninjutsu Uncovered*. Wayne, PA: A-LIST, 2007.

[SaOr09]   A. Sacco, A. Ortéga. "Persistant BIOS Infection." *Phrack*. Issue 66. 6 November 2009.
              http://www.phrack.com/issues.html?issue=66&id=7

[SP800-57]   NIST SP 800-57, *Recommendation for Key Management – Part 1: General*. March 2007.

[SP800-61]   NIST SP 800-61rev1, *Computer Security Incident Handling Guide*. March 2008.

[SP800-89]   NIST SP 800-89, *Recommendation for Obtaining Assurances for Digital Signature
              Applications*. November 2006.

[SP800-128]   Draft NIST SP 800-128, *Guide for Security Configuration Management of Information Systems.* March 2010.

[SP800-131A] NIST SP 800-131A, *Transitions: Recommendation for Transitioning the Use of Cryptographic Algorithms and Key Lengths.* January 2011.

[Sym02]   *W95.CIH Technical Details.* Symantec. 25 April 2002.
              http://www.symantec.com/security_response/writeup.jsp?docid=2000-122010-2655-99

[TCG05]   *PC Client Work Group Specific Implementation Specification for Conventional Bios Specification, Version 1.2.* Trusted Computing Group. July 2005.
              http://www.trustedcomputinggroup.org/resources/pc_client_work_group_specific_implementation_specification_for_conventional_bios_specification_version_12

[UEFI]   *UEFI Specification Version 2.3.* Unified EFI Forum. May 2009.
              http://www.uefi.org/specs/

[Wech09]   F. Wecherowski. "A Real SMM Rootkit: Reversing and Hooking BIOS SMI Handlers." *Phrack.* Issue 66. 6 November 2009.
              http://www.phrack.com/issues.html?issue=66&id=11

[WoTe09]   R. Wojtczuk and A. Tereshkin. "Attacking Intel BIOS." *Black Hat USA.* Las Vegas, NV. 30 July 2009. http://www.blackhat.com/presentations/bh-usa-09/WOJTCZUK/BHUSA09-Wojtczuk-AtkIntelBios-SLIDES.pdf